SOLAR
SYSTEM

Book

BY **KATHRYN** WHYMAN

SCIENCE WORKS

CONTENTS

THIS EDITION:
© 2016 Book Life
King's Lynn
Norfolk PE30 4HG

FIRST EDITION:
© Aladdin Books Ltd
PO Box 53987
London SW15 2SF

ISBN: 978-1-910512-12-8

All rights reserved.
Printed in Malaysia

A CIP record for this
book is available from
the British Library.

DESIGNED BY
Ian McMullen
EDITED BY
Grace Jones

INTRODUCTION

Look at the sky on a clear night and you can see thousands of stars. The universe contains millions more stars which are too far away to see. Our own part of this vast universe is called the Solar System. If we could travel from one side of the Solar System to the other it would take many years.

Not surprisingly, it has been difficult for scientists to find out about the Solar System. But in this book you will begin to understand something about it. You will find out about the Sun, the moons and conditions on the planets. You will learn how people have studied and are still studying the Solar System and where they think it came from.

TELESCOPES
ENABLE US TO
SEE FARAWAY
OBJECTS SUCH
AS GALAXIES.

WHAT IS THE SOLAR SYSTEM?

The Solar System is made up of the Sun, nine planets, several moons (the number changes as more are discovered) and a band of rocks called the Asteroid Belt. The planets and the Asteroid Belt all travel around the Sun. We say they 'orbit' the Sun. They each take a certain time to travel round the Sun. That time is a planet's 'year'. As the planets orbit, they themselves spin. They all spin at different speeds. The time they take to spin round once is called a 'day'. Many of the planets have moons. While the planets orbit the Sun, the moons orbit the planets.

You can see from the diagram that all the planets are different sizes. The Sun is so big compared to the planets that only a tiny part of it fits on the page!

PLANET	DISTANCE FROM THE SUN (MILLIONS KM)	DIAMETER (KM)	DAY LENGTH (EARTH DAYS/HOURS)	YEAR LENGTH (EARTH DAYS/YEARS)
Mercury	58	4,878	59 days	88 days
Venus	108	12,104	243 days	225 days
Earth	150	12,756	24 hours	365 days
Mars	228	6,794	24 1/2 hours	687 days
Jupiter	778	142,800	10 hours	12 years
Saturn	1,427	120,000	10 1/4 hours	29 1/2 years
Uranus	2,870	51,800	15 1/2 hours	84 years
Neptune	4,497	48,000	16 hours	165 years
Pluto	5,916	3,000	6 days 9 hours	248 years

As you can see from this table, the planets vary greatly in size and all are a very long way from the Sun. The planets closest to the Sun have the shortest years as they do not have as far to travel. The planets with the shortest days are the ones that spin round fastest.

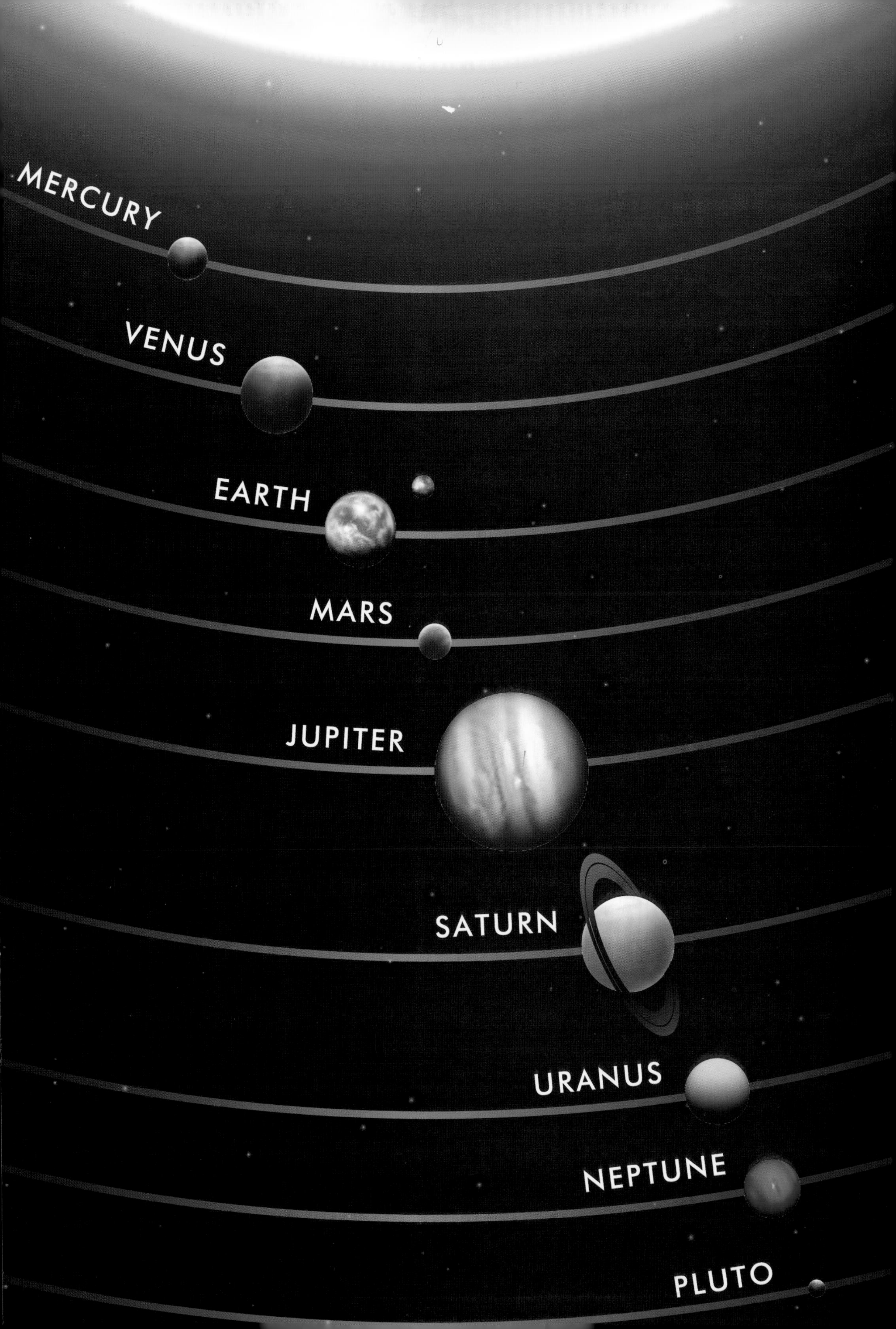

MERCURY

VENUS

EARTH

MARS

JUPITER

SATURN

URANUS

NEPTUNE

PLUTO

ORIGINS OF THE SOLAR SYSTEM

Scientists think that the Sun and planets grew out of a cloud of dust and gas about 4,600 million years ago. Part of this cloud collapsed and shrank and got very hot. This was the beginning of the Sun. The planets formed from the left-over gas and dust that circled the Sun.

Our Sun is a star. Stars form in enormous groups called 'galaxies'. Our Sun is part of the Milky Way galaxy. Stars are so far apart that we use special units called 'light years' to measure distances between them. Light travels faster than anything else in the universe. But light takes about 80,000 years to cross from one side of the Milky Way to the other! We say the Milky Way measures 80,000 light years across.

THE BIRTH OF THE SOLAR SYSTEM

These diagrams show how the Solar System probably began. The Sun formed first at the centre of the cloud (1-2). Specks of material bumped into each other and gradually built up into lumps (3). These grew to form the planets (4). Close to the Sun, where it was hottest, rocky planets grew. They had iron at their centres. These are the 'inner planets'. Further from the Sun, where it was cooler, gas planets grew. All the planets moved around the Sun.

THIS SPIRAL GALAXY AT THE TOP OF THE PHOTO IS A SIMILAR SHAPE TO OUR OWN GALAXY.

The Sun keeps the planets in their orbits. Like other stars, the Sun emits radiation in the form of heat, part of which is visible as light. Energy from the Sun is essential for life on Earth.

The Sun is huge. A hollow ball the size of the Sun could hold about a million Earths! It is also very hot. The surface of the Sun reaches about 6,000°C. The centre of the Sun is about 15 million degrees centigrade!

The Sun is made of the gases hydrogen and helium. At its centre, hydrogen is constantly being turned into helium. This is a nuclear reaction which releases huge amounts of energy. This energy travels to the surface of the Sun and then into space as radiation.

The surface of the Sun is called the 'photosphere'. Here there are often dark patches called 'sunspots'. These are areas of gas that are cooler than the rest of the surface. Although we call them spots, they are many times larger than the Earth. Giant jets of gas shoot out from the Sun, they are called 'flares'. Sometimes arches of gas loop across the surface. These are known as 'prominences'.

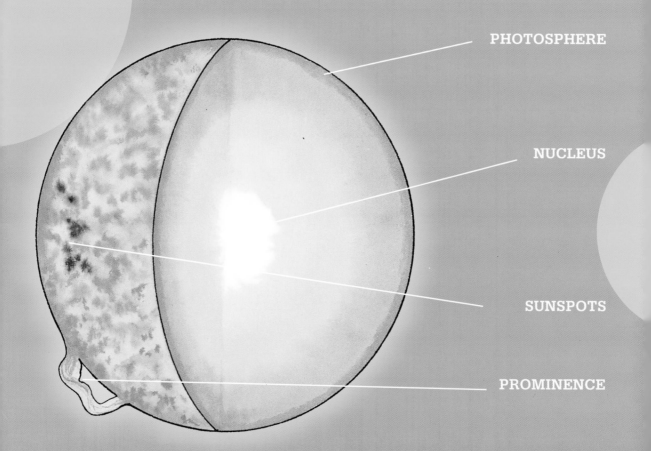

PHOTOSPHERE

NUCLEUS

SUNSPOTS

PROMINENCE

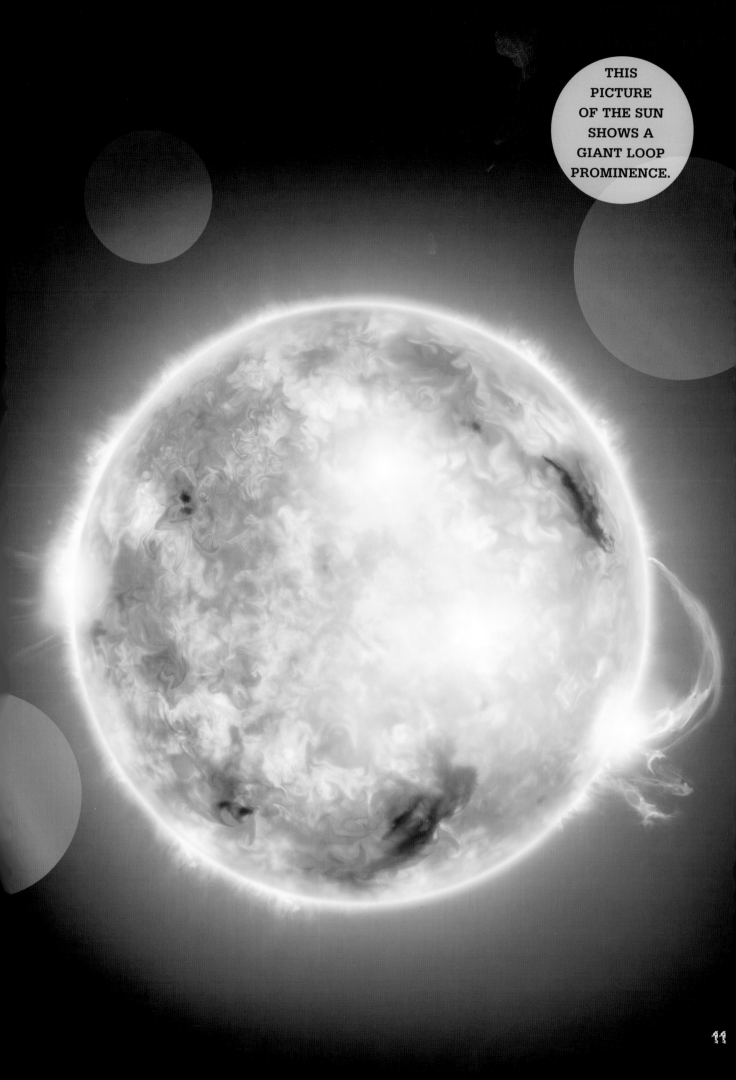

THIS PICTURE OF THE SUN SHOWS A GIANT LOOP PROMINENCE.

THE INNER PLANETS

The inner planets – Mercury, Venus, Earth and Mars – are all made of rock. They are quite small compared with some of the other planets. Mercury is closest to the Sun. It is extremely hot during the day but the temperature falls to -175°C at night. Mercury is only a little bigger than our Moon.

Although Venus is further from the Sun than Mercury, it is the hottest planet in the Solar System. Venus spins in the opposite direction to all the other planets. It also spins so slowly that its 'day' is longer than its 'year'!

Earth has water, oxygen and moderate temperatures. Because of this it can support life. Mars is about half the diameter of Earth. Temperatures here are never above 0°C and the only water is ice at the frozen poles.

MERCURY

LIKE THE MOON, THE SURFACE OF MERCURY IS PITTED WITH CRATERS AND COVERED IN DUST AND STONES. THERE IS NO AIR OR WATER. IT IS BATHED IN DANGEROUS RADIATION FROM THE SUN.

VENUS

ON THE SURFACE OF VENUS THERE ARE DEEP CRACKS AND DEAD VOLCANOES. THE ATMOSPHERE IS THICK WITH CARBON DIOXIDE GAS AND THE PLANET IS SURROUNDED BY CLOUDS OF SULPHURIC ACID.

MARS

MARS IS MADE OF RED ROCKS. IT HAS CRATERS AND DEAD VOLCANOES ON ITS SURFACE. THE ATMOSPHERE IS DUSTY AND MADE OF CARBON DIOXIDE. THERE ARE STRONG WINDS WHICH BLOW UP DUST STORMS.

EARTH

ABOUT THREE-QUARTERS OF THE EARTH'S SURFACE IS COVERED BY WATER. THE ATMOSPHERE CONTAINS THE GASES OXYGEN, NITROGEN AND A SMALL AMOUNT OF CARBON DIOXIDE.

THE GIANT PLANETS

Jupiter and Saturn are the two largest and fastest spinning planets in the Solar System. They are both made mostly of the gases hydrogen and helium. Jupiter is the largest. It weighs two and a half times as much as all the other planets put together. Its outer layer of gas clouds are about 1,000 km thick. Fierce winds blow these clouds and huge streaks of lightning flash between them. Below the cloud layer the gases get denser and denser until they become liquid.

Saturn is made of less dense gases; it could even float on water! The planet looks beautiful as it is surrounded by rings. The rings aren't solid. They are probably made of pieces of rock and ice which orbit the planet.

JUPITER

IO

EUROPA

HERE WE SEE JUPITER WITH 4 OF ITS MOONS. IT HAS AT LEAST 39 MOONS IN TOTAL.

GANYMEDE

CALLISTO

IAPETUS

TITAN

RHEA

DIONE

TETHYS

ENCELADUS

MIMAS

THIS IS AN ILLUSTRATION OF SATURN AND SEVERAL OF ITS MOONS.

THE OUTER PLANETS

Uranus, Neptune and Pluto are the planets furthest from the Sun. They get very little of the Sun's radiation so they are all dark and cold places. Uranus and Neptune are large planets made of gas. They look greeny-blue because they contain a gas called methane. Uranus is circled by nine rings, which are smaller than the rings around Saturn. The rings seem to be made of rocks and ice. Pluto is the greatest mystery of all. It was only discovered in 1930 and is even smaller than our Moon. It is probably made of rock and covered in ice. Pluto is usually the outermost planet. But sometimes its orbit crosses Neptune's for a period of 20 years, and then Neptune is the outermost planet. This last happened in 1979.

THIS ARTWORK SHOWS THE VOYAGER 2 SPACE PROBE AS IT PASSES NEPTUNE'S NORTH POLE.

AN ARTIST'S IMPRESSION OF URANUS AND ONE OF ITS MANY MOONS – IT HAS AT LEAST 22 MOONS.

A COMPUTER-GENERATED ILLUSTRATION OF THE PLANET PLUTO AND ITS MOON CHARON.

Originally Pluto – discovered in 1930 – was classified as the ninth planet in the Solar System. In 2006 it was reclassified as a 'dwarf planet' – a planet that has a lower mass than others within its orbit. There are now only eight recognised planets in the Solar System.

THE MOONS

A moon is a ball of rock that orbits a planet. Mercury and Venus are the only planets that do not have moons. Jupiter and Saturn each have at least 16 moons. Our Moon is our closest neighbour in space. Moons may be lumps of material that were left over when the planets formed. Like planets, moons can only be seen when they are lit up by the Sun.

We know more about our own Moon than any other member of the Solar System, apart from the Earth. Astronauts have even landed on the Moon. The Moon is a bare, dead place where nothing lives or grows. Its surface has hills and mountains as well as flat plains and deep craters. There is no water or air on the Moon and it is covered with a layer of fine dust. From the Moon, the sky always looks black and the Earth seems to change shape and go through phases.

PHASES OF THE MOON

Our Moon takes 27 1/2 days to orbit the Earth. During this time it seems to change shape. This is because only the side of the Moon that faces the Sun is lit up. And as the Moon orbits the Earth we see different amounts of this lit up side.

When the Moon is between the Sun and the Earth we cannot see it. This is called a 'New Moon'. A 'Full Moon' is when the Earth is between the Sun and the Moon. The diagrams show phases of the Moon seen in the Northern Hemisphere.

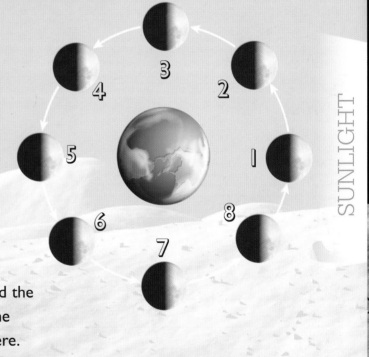

SUNLIGHT

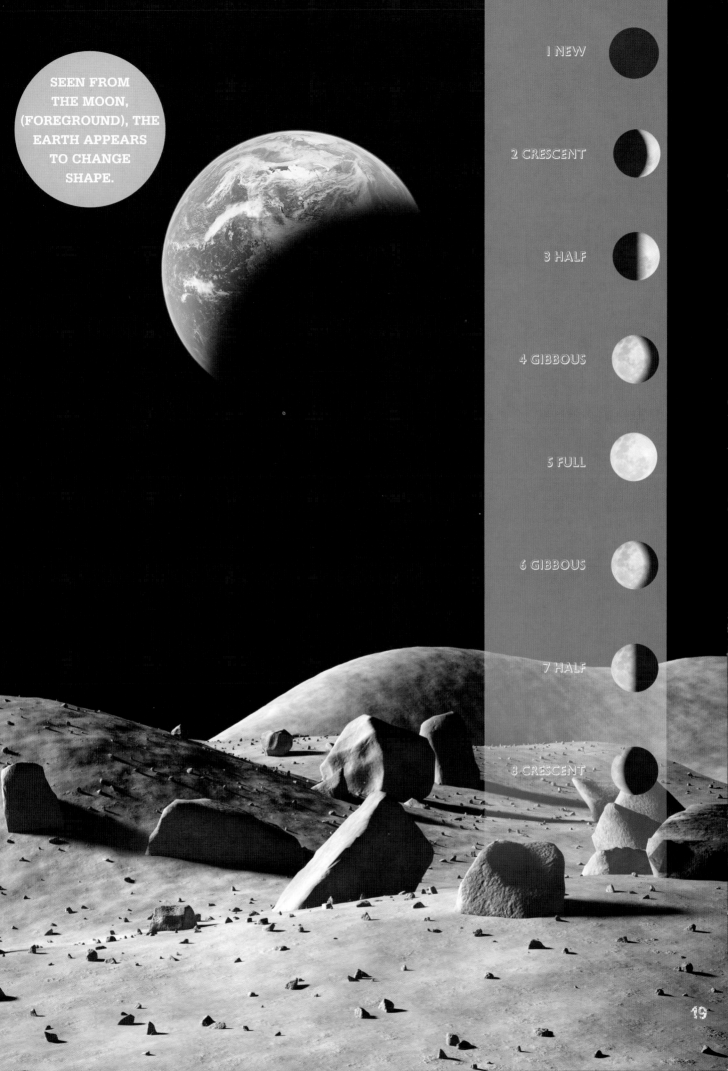

SEEN FROM THE MOON, (FOREGROUND), THE EARTH APPEARS TO CHANGE SHAPE.

1 NEW

2 CRESCENT

3 HALF

4 GIBBOUS

5 FULL

6 GIBBOUS

7 HALF

8 CRESCENT

FORCES IN THE SOLAR SYSTEM

The planets travel round the Sun in nearly circular paths. They are constantly changing direction. A force called 'gravity' makes the planets turn. You will have felt the force of the Earth's gravity – without it you would float up into space! Gravity is a force which pulls. All the planets exert gravity. The larger and heavier the planet, the stronger their pull of gravity becomes. The Sun is so massive that its gravity is strong enough to keep all the planets turning around it. Without this force, they would each fly off in a straight line.

The Moon also has gravity. Because it is smaller than the Earth, its pull of gravity is weaker – as the astronauts that landed on the Moon found out!

FORCES

Like the planets, this ball will keep moving in a circle as long as it travels fast enough. The force that acts along the string pulls the ball and makes it change direction. Although a different kind of force, its effect can be compared to the gravity exerted by the Sun. If the child let go of the string, there would be no pulling force to keep the ball turning. It would fly away in a straight line.

AN ASTRONAUT ON THE MOON'S SURFACE SALUTING THE US FLAG.

VISITORS TO THE SOLAR SYSTEM

Occasionally we see unknown objects in our Solar System. A comet is a ball made of rock and ice. This nucleus is surrounded by a cloud of gas called a 'coma'. When comets move close enough to the Sun, they reflect the Sun's light and form a tail of gas and dust.

Sometimes lumps of rock or metal from space crash to the Earth. These are 'meteorites'. A large meteorite may make a crater where it lands. Meteorites probably caused the craters on the surface of the Moon, Mercury and Mars – as well as this one in Arizona.

Comets leave bits of dust from their tails behind in space. Some of this dust enters the Earth's atmosphere where it burns up. We may then see a shower of bright 'shooting stars'. The scientific name for a shooting star is a 'meteor'.

THIS METEOR CRATER IN ARIZONA IS OVER 1 KILOMETRE WIDE AND 175 METRES DEEP.

HALLEY'S COMET

Halley's comet is a regular visitor to our part of the Solar System. It returns about every 76 years and has been seen throughout the ages. The diagram shows the strange shape of the comet's orbit – a long oval. The comet is invisible beyond Saturn's orbit. You can see how the comet's tail always points away from the Sun.

23

OBSERVING THE SOLAR SYSTEM

The planets and stars are far too far away to see clearly, however good your eyesight is. The telescope was invented to help people look at faint, distant objects and see them in more detail. Telescopes collect more light than the human eye. They can also make things look bigger. Stars looked at through a telescope seem to be brighter and closer.

Telescopes use either a lens or a mirror to collect light and focus it. Another lens is used to produce a magnified image. Modern telescopes are housed in giant buildings called 'observatories'. These are often built at the top of a mountain where there is a clear view of the sky.

THE TELESCOPE

This telescope uses one convex lens to collect and focus light, and another to magnify the image. Sliding the outer tube changes the distance between the two lenses. This is important as it allows you to see objects that are near and far away.

WARNING! THE LIGHT OF THE SUN CAN BE BLINDING. NEVER LOOK DIRECTLY AT THE SUN.

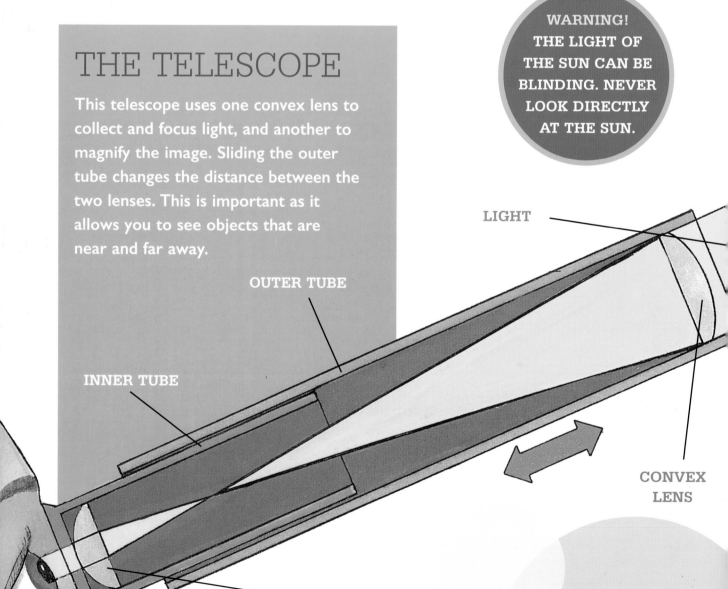

LIGHT

OUTER TUBE

INNER TUBE

CONVEX LENS

CONVEX LENS

24

LOOKING DOWN ON A TELESCOPE IN THE OBSERVATORY AT KITT PEAK, ARIZONA, USA.

EXPLORING THE SOLAR SYSTEM

Watching the Solar System from the Earth is one way of finding out about it. To learn more, people have used rockets to travel into space. There they have been able to look at parts of the Solar System more clearly. Although the first men landed on the Moon in 1969, no one has visited any of the planets. They are too far away and conditions are dangerous for humans.

However, space probes – robot controlled unmanned spacecraft – have been sent far into the Solar System. The space probe Voyager 2 has travelled through the Solar System and is now well beyond the orbit of Pluto. As it travels it takes pictures and sends them back to Earth.

CAMERAS AND DETECTORS

RADIO DISH

FUEL

ANTENNAE

NUCLEAR GENERATOR

VOYAGER 2

This is a diagram of Voyager 2. This space probe has already travelled across millions of kilometres of space, and has collected information on Jupiter, Saturn, Uranus and Neptune. The craft's onboard computers are reprogrammed during its flight by electronic signals from Earth. The entire vehicle weighs only 815 kilograms. It carries equipment for 11 scientific experiments which are powered by a nuclear generator.

THE SURFACE OF MARS – YOU CAN SEE THE SOLAR PANELS OF THE LANDER AT THE BOTTOM OF THE PHOTO.

THIS IS A PHOTOGRAPH OF THE SURFACE OF MARS.

MAKE YOUR OWN MOBILE

You can have the Solar System hanging from your ceiling! This mobile is easy to make. It will help you remember some of the things you have learnt about the Solar System.

Trace the shapes of the members of the Solar System onto card and cut them out. Fit the rings around Saturn, Jupiter and Uranus. Use the diagram below to measure lengths of strong cotton. Remember to cut them longer so you have enough to fix the ends. Fix each piece of cotton to the top of its planet. Hang the planets from the Sun and colour them, as shown in the diagram. Attach cotton to either end of the Sun and your mobile is now ready to hang.

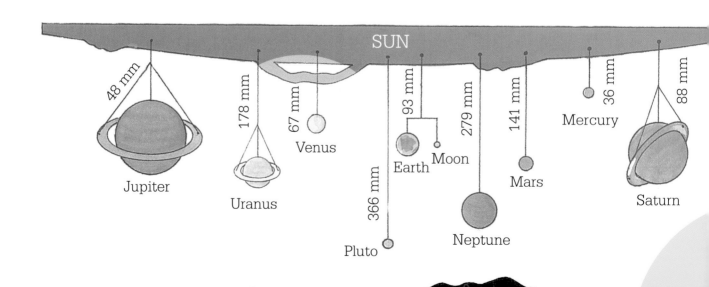

SUN

48 mm — Jupiter
178 mm — Uranus
67 mm — Venus
93 mm — Earth
Moon
366 mm — Pluto
279 mm — Neptune
141 mm — Mars
36 mm — Mercury
88 mm — Saturn

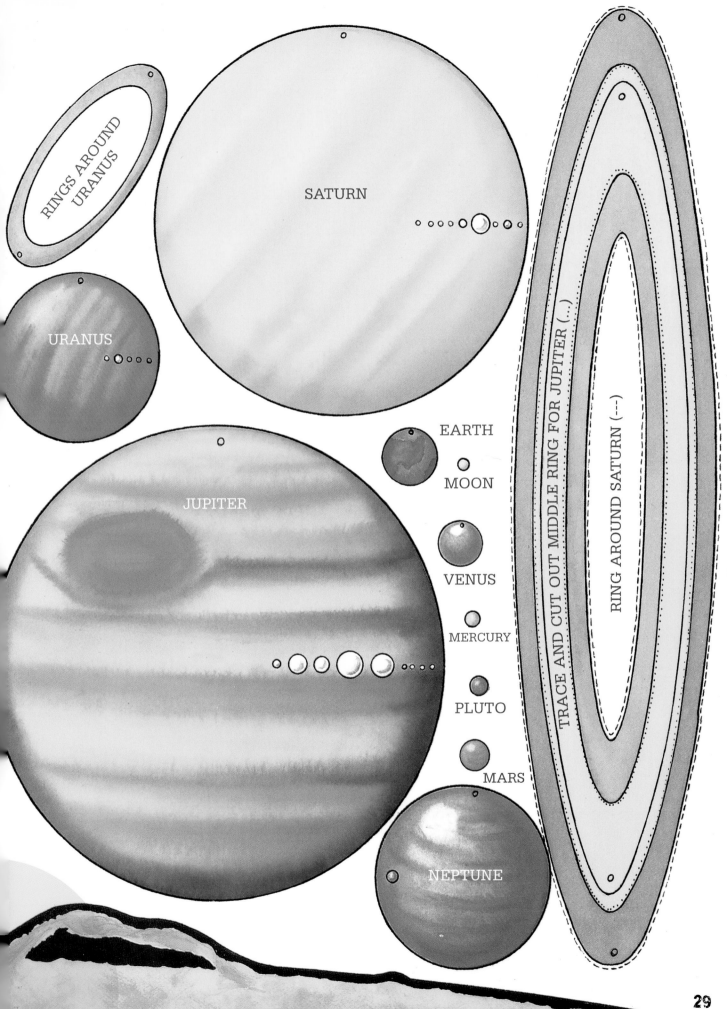

RINGS AROUND URANUS

SATURN

URANUS

JUPITER

EARTH

MOON

VENUS

MERCURY

PLUTO

MARS

NEPTUNE

TRACE AND CUT OUT MIDDLE RING FOR JUPITER (...)

RING AROUND SATURN (---)

SUN

29

LIFE AND DEATH OF A STAR

When a star like our Sun first forms it is different from the way we see it today. At first the Sun was a very hot, blue star. As it grew bigger it cooled down and looked white. The Sun will shine as it is for about 10,000 million years. Eventually it will swell and form a 'Red Giant'. Some of the stars we see are Red Giants. They are cooler than the Sun. But as they are many times bigger, they appear brighter. A Red Giant slowly cools and shrinks. Its outer layers of gas drift away and a small hot star called a 'White Dwarf' is left. This slowly cools and becomes a 'Black Dwarf'.

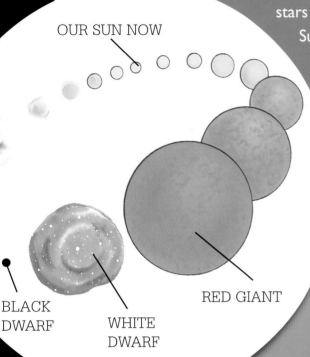

OUR SUN NOW

BLACK
DWARF

WHITE
DWARF

RED GIANT

VERY LARGE STARS

Stars much bigger than our Sun also become Red Giants, but they blow up in a huge explosion called a 'supernova'. They shrink into themselves and form a 'Black Hole'. Anything nearby gets sucked into a black hole. Even its own light cannot escape!

GLOSSARY

ASTEROID
A piece of rock floating in space. The Asteroid Belt is a band of thousands of asteroids that orbit the Sun between Mars and Jupiter.

ASTRONAUT
Someone who travels in space.

ASTRONOMER
A scientist who studies the stars, planets and galaxies.

ATMOSPHERE
A thin blanket of gases which surrounds a planet. The gases are held in place by the gravity of the planet.

BLACK HOLE
A collapsed star whose gravity is so strong that not even light can escape its pull.

GALAXY
A group of millions of stars. Galaxies can be different shapes and sizes. There are millions of them in the Universe.

GRAVITY
The pulling force of attraction between two objects. The bigger and heavier an object, the greater its force of gravity.

IMAGE
The picture of an object which you see when you look at it through a lens or in a mirror.

LIGHT YEAR
This is a unit of distance. It is the distance that light travels in one Earth year. It is equal to 9 1/2 million million kilometres.

MAGNIFY
Make something look bigger than it really is.

MOON
A ball of rock that orbits a planet.

PLANET
A big ball of substances (such as rocks, liquids and gases) that orbits the Sun.

RADIATION
Movement of light, and other rays, from hot bodies such as the Sun through space to the planets.

RED GIANT
An old star whose core has collapsed and heated, forcing its outer layers to expand – sometimes as much as 300 times the size of the Sun.

ROCKET
A very powerful engine that can be used to lift spacecraft and satellites into space.

SPACE PROBES
Unmanned spacecraft sent to study other planets.

STAR
A gigantic ball of very hot gases which glows. The Sun is a star.

SUPERNOVA
The massive explosion of a dying star which shines billions of times brighter than an ordinary star.

UNIVERSE
Everything that exists, including the Solar System, our galaxy (the Milky Way) and all the other millions of galaxies. Scientists think the Universe is getting larger all the time.

WHITE DWARF
The stage after a star has been a Red Giant. White Dwarfs have run out of fuel and are dying.

INDEX

PHOTOGRAPHIC CREDITS
Abbreviations: l-left, r-right, b-bottom, t-top, c-centre, m-middle

Front cover — solarseven/shutterstock.com. 2-3 — Johan Swanepoel/shutterstock.com. 4-5 — Maria Starovoytova/shutterstock.com. 6, 21, 26 — Vadim Sadovski/shutterstock.com. 7 — fluidworkshop/shutterstock.com. 8-9 — njaj/shutterstock.com. 11 — solarseven/shutterstock.com. 12bc — NASA & NSSDC. 12tr — Ksanawo/shutterstock.com. 13tr — jupeart/shutterstock.com. 13bc — Triff/shutterstock.com. 14 — Kirschner/shutterstock.com. 15 — fluidworkshop/shutterstock.com. 16bl — David Hardy/Astro Art. 16tr, 23 — Corbis. 17 — Aphelleon/shutterstock.com. 18-19 — hkeita/shutterstock.com. 20 — Ralf Juergen Kraft/shutterstock.com. 22 — bjsites/shutterstock.com. 25 — Colorific. 27br — NASA. 30 — Lonely/shutterstock.com.